OPRAH WINFREY.
THE LITTLE BLACK BOOK

"MAY THE WISDOM OF THE GREATEST MINDS
BECOME YOURS."
S. C. HOLLISTER

RENEGADE PUBLISHING

OPRAH WINFREY. The Little Black Book
Design Copyright © 2015 S.C. Hollister
Published by Renegade Publishing
California

To Oprah Winfrey,
Thank you.

Contents

The Little Black Book used to be a means of getting in touch with people who could give you what you wanted; most famously understood as a Booty Call book.

But, in this 21ST century version of the little black book, wisdom and knowledge are the key to opening doors.

The design of this book invites you to meditate on the wisdom within, have focused conversations, or protect your coffee table from condensation.

May the wisdom of some of the greatest, become yours.

OPRAH WINFREY.
THE LITTLE BLACK BOOK

Oprah's Little Black Book

~

1. "The greatest discovery of all time is that a person can change his future by merely changing his attitude."

2. "If you want to accomplish the goals of your life, you have to begin with the spirit."

3. "With every experience, you alone are painting your own canvas, thought by thought, choice by choice."

4. "The more you praise and celebrate your life, the more there is in life to celebrate."

5. "We can't become what we need to be by remaining what we are."

6. "Surround yourself with only people who are going to lift you higher. Life is already filled with those who want to bring you down."

7. "You can have it all. Just not all at once."

8. "Think like a queen. A queen is not afraid to fail. Failure is another steppingstone to greatness."

9. "Go ahead, fall down. The world looks different from the ground."

10. "Where there is no struggle, there is no strength."

11. "Turn your wounds into wisdom."

12. "If you don't know what your passion is, realize that one reason for your existence on earth is to find it."

13. "The big secret in life is that there is no big secret. Whatever your goal, you can get there if you're willing to work."

14. "It doesn't matter who you are, where you came from. The ability to triumph begins with you. Always."

15. "Books were my pass to personal freedom. I learned to read at age three, and soon discovered there was a whole world to conquer that went beyond our farm in Mississippi."

16. "As you become more clear about who you really are, you'll be better able to decide what is best for you – the first time around."

17. "Follow your instincts. That is where true wisdom manifests itself."

18. "Spirituality means living your life with an open heart to kindness, grace, gratitude, forgiveness, faith, courage, truth, love and ultimately Divine Law."

19. "I trust that everything happens for a reason, even when we're not wise enough to see it."

20. "Failure is a great teacher, if you're open to it."

21. "Use your life to serve the world, and you will find that is also serves you."

22. "When someone shows you who they are, believe them the first time."

23. "Lots of people want to ride with you in the limo, but what you want is someone who will take the bus with you when the limo breaks down."

24. "The struggle of my life created empathy – I could relate to pain, being abandoned, having people not love me."

25. "I know for sure that what we dwell on is who we become."

26. "Real integrity is doing the right thing, knowing that nobody's going to know whether you did it or not."

27. "I am a woman in process. I'm just trying like everybody else. I try to take every conflict, every experience, and learn from it. Life is never dull."

28. "What I know is, is that if you do work that you love, and the work fulfills you, the rest will come."

29. "I don't think of myself as a poor deprived ghetto girl who made good. I think of myself as somebody who from an early age knew I was responsible for myself, and I had to make good."

30. "Don't back down just to keep the peace. Standing up for your beliefs builds self-confidence and self-esteem."

31. "Let excellence be your brand… when you are excellent, you become unforgettable. Doing the right thing, even when nobody knows you're doing the right thing will always bring the right thing to you."

32. "Only make decisions that support your self-image, self-esteem, and self-worth."

33. "I was once afraid of people saying, 'Who does she think she is?' Now I have the courage to stand and say, 'This is who I am.'"

34. "Do the one thing you think you cannot do. Fail at it. Try again. Do better the second time. The only people who never tumble are those who never mount the high wire. This is your moment. Own it."

35. "Breathe. Let go. And remind yourself that this very moment is the only one you know you have for sure."

36. "The biggest adventure you can take is to live the life of your dreams."

37. "Happiness is a living thing... you have to feed it."

38. "Sometimes you find out what you are supposed to be doing by doing the things you are not supposed to do."

39. "I ALWAYS KNEW I WAS DESTINED FOR GREATNESS."

40. "IF YOU WANT YOUR LIFE TO BE MORE REWARDING, YOU HAVE TO CHANGE THE WAY YOU THINK."

41. "I'VE COME TO BELIEVE THAT EACH OF US HAS A PERSONAL CALLING THAT'S AS UNIQUE AS A FINGERPRINT, THAT THE BEST WAY TO SUCCEED IS TO DISCOVER WHAT YOU LOVE, AND THEN FIND A WAY TO OFFER IT TO OTHERS IN THE FORM OF SERVICE, WORKING HARD, AND ALSO ALLOWING THE ENERGY OF THE UNIVERSE TO LEAD YOU."

42. "I THINK THE WHOLE WORLD WOULD BE A BETTER PLACE IF EVERYONE LOVED EACH OTHER A LITTLE MORE."

43. "When I look into the future, it's so bright it burns my eyes."

44. "Passion is energy. Feel the power that comes from focusing on what excites you."

45. "You get in life what you have the courage to ask for."

46. "I finally realized that being grateful to my body was key to giving more love to myself."

47. "It isn't until you come to a spiritual understanding of who you are – not necessarily a religious feeling, but deep down, the spirit within – that you can begin to take control."

48. "I had no idea that being your authentic self could make me as rich as I've become. If I had, I'd have done it a lot earlier."

49. "Duct tape is like the Force. It has a light side, a dark side and it holds the Universe together."

50. "Unless you choose to do great things with it, it makes no difference how much you are rewarded, or how much power you have."

51. "When your life is on course with its purpose, you are your most powerful."

52. "You know you are on the road to success if you would do your job, and not be paid for it."

53. "Nobody but you is responsible for your life. It doesn't matter what your Mama did, it doesn't matter what your Daddy didn't do. You are responsible for your life. You are responsible for the energy that you create for yourself, and you are responsible for the energy that you bring to others."

54. "If you look at what you have in life, you will always have more. If you look at what you do not have in life, you will never have enough."

55. "Doing the best at this moment puts you in the best place for the next moment."

56. "Biology is the least of what makes someone a mother."

57. "For every one of us that succeeds, it's because there's somebody there to show you the way out. The light doesn't always necessarily have to be in your family; for me it was teachers and school."

58. "Luck is a matter of preparation meeting opportunity."

59. "I do not believe in failure. It is not failure if you enjoyed the process."

60. "You cannot hate other people without hating yourself."

61. "I don't want anyone who doesn't want me."

62. "The thing you fear most has no power. Your fear of it is what has the power. Facing the truth really will set you free."

63. "I used to not think it was worth the trouble to make a beautiful cup of tea. Now I know I'm worth the trouble and so, I make a beautiful cup."

64. "I would like to thank the people who've brought me those dark moments, when I felt most wounded, betrayed. You have been my greatest teachers."

65. "One of the hardest things in life to learn is which bridges to cross and which bridges to burn."

66. "I have a lot of things to prove to myself. One is that I can live my life fearlessly."

67. "Don't settle for a relationship that won't let you be yourself."

68. "Create the highest grandest vision possible for your life, because you become what you believe."

69. "What I know for sure is this: You are built not to shrink down to less, but to blossom into more. To be more splendid. To be more extraordinary."

70. "Understand that the right to choose your own path is a sacred privilege. Use it. Dwell in possibility."

71. "There is a lesson in almost everything that you do, and getting the lesson is how you move forward. It is how you enrich your spirit."

72. "When you undervalue what you do, the world will undervalue who you are."

73. "Excellence is the best deterrent to racism or sexism."

74. "There is no greater gift you can give or receive than to honor your calling. It's why you were born. And how you become most truly alive."

75. "You do not become what you want. You become what you believe."

76. "The great courageous act that we must all do is to have the courage to step out of our history and past so that we can live our dreams."

77. "You are responsible for your life. You can't keep blaming somebody else for your dysfunction. Life is really about moving on."

78. "Alone time is when I distance myself from the voices of the world so I can hear my own."

79. "I will tell you that there have been no failures in my life. I don't want to sound like some metaphysical queen, but there have been no failures. There have been some tremendous lessons."

80. "I want every day to be a fresh start on expanding what is possible."

81. "Life is about becoming more of who you really are."

82. "What God intended for you goes far beyond anything you can imagine."

83. "The whole point of being alive is to evolve into the complete person you were intended to be."

84. "Challenges are gifts that force us to search for a new center of gravity. Don't fight them. Just find a new way to stand."

85. "Failure is a signpost to turn you in another direction."

86. "If you make a choice that goes against what everyone else thinks, the world will not fall apart."

87. "There is no feud. It's only peace and love."

88. "Every day brings a chance for you to draw in a breath, kick of your shoes, and dance."

89. "Do what you have to do until you can do what you want to do."

90. "I believe that one of life's greatest risks is never daring to risk."

91. "You have to find what sparks a light in you so that you in your own way, can illuminate the world."

92. "I remember a specific moment, watching my grandmother hang the clothes on the line, and her saying to me, 'You are going to have to learn to do this,' and me being in that space of awareness and knowing that my life would not be the same as my grandmother's life."

93. "Love is a verb. Is there admiration and respect? If there isn't, then there is no love. Love is not a feeling, it is behavior, it is how a person acts and how they treat you."

94. "You can't be friends with someone who wants your life."

95. "The best of times is now."

96. "The chance to love and be loved exists no matter where you are."

97. "There is a difference, you know, between thinking you deserve to be happy and knowing you are worthy of happiness."

98. "I still have my feet on the ground, I just wear better shoes."

99. "True forgiveness is when you can say, 'Thank you for that experience.'"

100. "At the roll call of your life, at the end of your life, what really matters is who did you love and who did you offer love to."

101. "I consider this world to be like a school and our lives to be the classrooms."

102. "It makes no difference how many peaks you reach if there was no pleasure in the climb."

103. "I am where I am because of the bridges that I crossed. Sojourner Truth was a bridge. Ida B. Wells was a bridge. Madame C. J. Walker was a bridge. Fannie Lou Hamer was a bridge."

104. "Your true passion should feel like breathing; it's that natural."

105. "Nothing happens until you decide. Make a decision and watch your life move forward."

106. "In the midst of difficulty, lies opportunity."

107. "What material success does is provide you with the ability to concentrate on other things that really matter. And that is being able to make a difference, not only in your own life, but in other people's lives."

108. "I believe that every single event in life happens in an opportunity to choose love over fear."

109. "If you want your life to be more rewarding, you have to change the way you think."

110. "Start making the best out of the life you are living with two simple words: I AM."

111. "In order to get people's attention you got to blow a loud trumpet, you got to beat the drum loudly. Nobody listens to you when you go quietly into the night."

112. "I don't think you ever stop giving. I really don't. I think it's an on-going process. And it's not just about being able to write a check. It's about being able to touch somebody's life."

113. "Create the highest, grandest vision for your life. Then let every step move you in that direction."

114. "Forgiveness is letting go of the hope that the past can be changed."

115. "Living in the moment means letting go of the past and not waiting for the future. It means living your life consciously, aware that each moment you breathe is a gift."

116. "I believe that the only courage anybody ever needs is the courage to follow your own dreams."

117. "Know what you want, and be willing to work as hard as anybody who's ever lived, to get it."

118. "Running is the greatest metaphor for life, because you get out of it what you put into it."

119. "Being still at least once a day will enhance your life."

120. "This year I am choosing to live beyond my wildest dreams. I wonder where they'll take me."

121. "No experience is ever wasted. Everything has meaning."

122. "It's much easier for me to make major life, multi-million dollar decisions, than it is to decide on a carpet for my front porch. That's the truth."

123. "My idea of heaven is a great big baked potato and someone to share it with."

124. "Nobody's journey is seamless or smooth. We all stumble. We all have setbacks. It's just life's way of saying, 'time to change course.'"

125. "It does not matter how you came into the world. What matters is that you are here."

126. "I'm sick of people sittin' in chairs stating their problems. Then we roll the videotape… then we have our experts on the topic… I'm in the 'What's next?' phase of my career."

127. "If you come to fame not understanding who you are, it will define who you are."

128. "Gratitude is the single greatest treasure I will take with me from this experience."

129. "I define joy as a sustained sense of well-being and internal peace – a connection to what matters."

130. "I don't yell at people. I don't mistreat people. I don't talk down to people. So no one else in this building, in this vicinity, has the right to do it."

131. "You are responsible for your life. If you're sitting around waiting on somebody to save you, to fix you, to even help you, you are wasting your time. Only you have the power to move your life forward."

132. "I've talked to nearly 30,000 people on this show, and all 30,000 had one thing in common: They all wanted validation… I would tell you that every single person you will ever meet shares that common desire."

133. "When you're doing the work you're meant to do, it feels right and every day is a bonus, regardless of what you're getting paid."

134. "How do I define success? Let me tell you, money's pretty nice. But having a lot of money does not automatically make you a successful person. What you want is money and meaning. You want your work to be meaningful, because meaning is what brings the real richness to your life."

135. "I believe the choice to be excellent begins with aligning your thoughts and words with the intention to require more from yourself."

136. "Challenges are gifts that force us to search for a new center of gravity. Don't fight them. Just find a different way to stand."

137. "Every time you state what you want or believe, you're the first to hear it. It's a message to both you and others about what you think is possible. Don't put a ceiling on yourself."

138. "Forget about the fast lane. If you really want to fly, harness your power to your passion. Honor your calling. Everybody has one. Trust your heart, and success will come to you."

139. "You get to know who you really are in a crisis."

140. "Living in the moment brings you a sense of reverence for all of life's blessings."

141. "If someone wants you, nothing can keep him away. If he doesn't want you, nothing can make him stay. Stop trying to change yourself for a relationship that's not meant to be... Slower is better. Never live your life for someone before you find what makes you truly happy."

142. "Devote today to something so daring even you cannot believe you're doing it!"

...

More Titles in *The Little Black Book* series:

Alaska Noon
Albert Einstein
Benjamin Franklin
Bill Gates
Bruce Lee
Buddha
Elon Musk
Ida B. Wells
Jesus Christ
Johnny Depp
Jon Stewart
Mahatma Gandhi
Mark Zuckerberg
Martin Luther King Jr.
Nicholas Cage
Nikola Tesla
Richard Branson
Russell Brand
Steve Jobs
Steven Colbert
Walt Disney

If there is someone you'd like to see added to *The Little Black Book* series, please leave a comment in this books review section on Amazon.com.

Printed in Great Britain
by Amazon